D0932534

HOLIDAY HISTORIES

THE STORY BEHIND
ST. PATRICK'S DAY

JACK READER

PowerKiDS press.

New York

Published in 2020 by The Rosen Publishing Group, Inc.
29 East 21st Street, New York, NY 10010

Copyright © 2020 by The Rosen Publishing Group, Inc.

All rights reserved. No part of this book may be reproduced in any form without permission in writing from the publisher, except by a reviewer.

First Edition

Editor: Tanya Dellaccio
Book Design: Reann Nye

Photo Credits: Cover, pp. 1, 15, 19, 22 Stuart Monk/Shutterstock.com; pp. 4, 6, 8, 12, 14, 16, 18, 20, 22 (background) Preto Perola/Shutterstock.com; p. 5 Liviu Toader/Shutterstock.com; p. 7 Bettmann/Getty Images; p. 9 https://commons.wikimedia.org/wiki/File:Saint_Patrick_Catholic_Church_(Junction_City,_Ohio)_-_stained_glass,_Saint_Patrick_-_detail.jpg; p. 11 NurPhoto/Getty Images; p. 13 Everett Historical/Shutterstock.com; p. 16 Hector Rodriguez / EyeEm /Getty Images; p. 17 D Guest Smith/Shutterstock.com; p. 21 Brent Hofacker/Shutterstock.com.

Cataloging-in-Publication Data

Names: Reader, Jack.
Title: The story behind St. Patrick's Day / Jack Reader.
Description: New York : PowerKids Press, 2020. | Series: Holiday histories | Includes glossary and index.
Identifiers: ISBN 9781725300606 (pbk.) | ISBN 9781725300620 (library bound) | ISBN 9781725300613 (6pack)
Subjects: LCSH: Saint Patrick's Day–Juvenile literature.
Classification: LCC GT4995.P3 R43 2020 | DDC 394.262–dc23

Manufactured in the United States of America

CPSIA Compliance Information: Batch #CSPK19. For Further Information contact Rosen Publishing, New York, New York at 1-800-237-9932.

RICHMOND HILL PUBLIC LIBRARY
32972001666355 RV
The story behind St. Patrick's Day
Nov.. 25, 2019

CONTENTS

A Special Celebration

Every year on March 17, people dress up in green to **celebrate** St. Patrick's Day. St. Patrick was a **saint** in Ireland in the fifth century. The holiday is full of parades, **traditional** food and drink, and parties. It's celebrated around the world!

St. Patrick

St. Patrick was born in Britain, but he spent many years of his life as a **slave** in Ireland. He was taken there against his will when he was 16 years old. He escaped and left Ireland in the 400s.

7

St. Patrick returned to Ireland years later to teach the people of Ireland about **Christianity**. He helped start churches and schools while he was there. Today, St. Patrick is known as the patron saint of Ireland. This means that he's said to guide Ireland and keep its people safe.

Giving Honor

St. Patrick died on March 17, 461. Years later, in 1631, the Catholic Church started a feast day on the **anniversary** of the day he died. People would go to a church service in St. Patrick's honor and have big meals with different foods.

Celebrating the Irish

In time, the church's feast day became a larger celebration—not only to honor St. Patrick but also to celebrate Ireland's history. In the 1700s, many Irish people began moving to the United States. They brought their traditions with them. These people created the St. Patrick's Day celebrations we know today.

Parades of People

New York City had its first St. Patrick's Day parade in 1762. Today, the city has the largest St. Patrick's Day parade in the United States. Families and friends get dressed up in green to sing, dance, and eat in honor of their Irish **heritage**.

ST. PATRICK'S DAY
17th March
2012
CARROLL'S

Going Green

The color green became linked with the holiday in 1798 when Irish soldiers started wearing green in battle. Starting in 1962, the city of Chicago has dyed its river green in support of the holiday every year. Green plants called shamrocks are also a **symbol** of the holiday.

shamrock

Chicago Tribune
DuSABLE BRIDGE
BIGBUS
Cityview

Keeping Traditions Alive

As more Irish people moved to the United States, the celebrations got bigger. There are many different Irish traditions at St. Patrick's Day parades, such as Irish dancing. People dress up in costumes and dance to traditional Irish music.

GAP

Corned beef and cabbage make up a now-traditional Irish meal that people eat on St. Patrick's Day. People even put dye in drinks to turn them green for the holiday. Many people wear shamrocks and green clothing as they celebrate.

Irish Importance

People often celebrate St. Patrick's Day with fun and colorful parties during which they celebrate their Irish roots. But it's important to remember that the day also honors the Irish **contribution** to the United States and the world. Today, thousands of people get together for parades in cities all over the world to celebrate!

GLOSSARY

anniversary: A day remembered or celebrated because something happened on that day in an earlier year.

celebrate: To do something special or enjoyable done for an important event or holiday.

Christianity: A religion based on the teachings of Jesus Christ.

contribution: Something that is contributed, or given.

heritage: The traditions or beliefs that are part of the history of a group or nation.

saint: A holy person recognized by a Christian church.

slave: Someone who is "owned" by another person.

symbol: Something that stands for something else.

traditional: Following what's been done for a long time.

INDEX

WEBSITES

Due to the changing nature of Internet links, PowerKids Press has developed an online list of websites related to the subject of this book. This site is updated regularly. Please use this link to access the list: www.powerkidslinks.com/HH/patrick